NEW YORK

Hey, welcome to New York City! You're one of 45 million visitors that flock here every year to enjoy all the incredible things there are to do and see.

If you're a thrill seeker, you can learn the flying trapeze or scream on a rollercoaster; but if you prefer culture and learning, there are terrific museums, kids' workshops and shows for you to enjoy. There are also interesting neighborhoods to explore, lots of yummy cuisines to taste, and stores that'll tempt the most reluctant shopper in your family.

So, what are you waiting for? Follow your guide dog, Go!

kidsGo! **Travel Guides**
Written by Mio Debnam
Illustrated by Tania Willis

HAVEN
BOOKS

Design Director: Timothy Jones / Designer: Katie Kwan
Published by Haven Books Ltd, Hong Kong
ISBN 978-988-18967-7-3
Copyright © 2011 by Haven Books Limited
www.havenbooksonline.com

NOTE TO OUR READERS: We try to recommend the best
attractions, restaurants and tour providers, using trusted
word-of-mouth recommendations; however, we cannot be held
responsible for the safety, scope and quality of their service.
We also strive to provide the most accurate information
possible, but of course, some things may have changed by
the time you visit. If you do notice anything inaccurate in our
guide, or think we've missed out on listing something really
good, please help us to make it better by letting us know about
it. We'd also love to hear from you about all the things you
liked or disliked during your trip, so we can continue to keep
our guides as up-to-date and reliable as possible.

How to tell us? Simply log on to the Family Feedback page at:
www.kidsgotravelguides.com

CONTENTS

SURVEY NEW YORK FROM THE TOP OF "THE ROCK"

Rockefeller Center, 30 Rockefeller Plaza (entrance on 50th St, between Fifth & Sixth Avenues) Tel: 1-877-692-7625

A fun thing to do in any city is to go somewhere really high to get a bird's eye view. In New York, the **Rockefeller Center** is a great place to do this! The observation decks are on the 67th, 69th and 70th floors – so the wrap-around view is spectacular! Take a photo of yourself with the **Empire State Building** or **Central Park** in the background – and blow a kiss to the **Statue of Liberty** while you're up there. However, before you get into the special glass-ceilinged elevator to go to the observation decks, spend a little time on the mezzanine level. Watch the short films about the

Before you start hitting the sights, ask your parents to check out www.citypass.com/new-york – you can get big discounts on a package of tickets to six great destinations, including Top of the Rock, museums, boat tours and more.

ST-DOS

history of Rockefeller Center, and try the 'beam walk' – which will give you some idea of how good the construction workers' sense of balance was! The best way to buy tickets, so you don't have to line up, is to buy them online (*www.topoftherocknyc.com/tickets*) or get a discount with a CityPASS if you plan to do a lot of sightseeing (see Go's advice, pg 4).

SEE THE SEA LIONS AT CENTRAL PARK ZOO

SE corner of Central Park, 64th St & Fifth Avenue Tel: 1-212-439-6500

There are tons of great things to do in Manhattan's Central Park, like boating, biking, swimming, sailing model boats, watching shows and plain having fun – see pgs 10, 14, 22, 58! But if you love animals, your first destination once you get to Central Park should be this little zoo in the middle of the city. It's far smaller than Bronx Zoo, but that's part of the charm – you can see all the best parts in a couple of hours and still have time to visit some other sights. As you enter the zoo, find out what time the sea lions get fed. Plan your visit so you can see the show if possible; they 'work' hard for their supper! There are lots of other animals to see: Polar bears, waddling penguins, tortoises, hornbills; monkeys, red pandas and snow leopards. There are 1,400 animals of 130 species in the zoo! If you love cuddling rabbits, pop into **Tisch Children's Zoo**, too. You'll be able to pet and feed sleepy pigs, friendly goats and other farm animals. This area is fantastic for those aged 6 and under. The zoo is open all year, from 10am. It closes at 5pm on weekdays, 5.30pm on weekends, and at 4.30pm from November 1st to April 1st.

GO TO A FUNFAIR ON CONEY ISLAND

Kids living in New York have been visiting Coney Island every summer for decades. Why? Because it's FUN! It has a **beach**, a **baseball stadium**, a **circus** (pg 18) and an **aquarium** (pg 13) as well as a bunch of amusement parks – some of which have rides that are over 90 years old! The rides are well looked after, but don't expect the parks to be all new and squeaky clean – this is a blast from the past and the look is 'vintage'. Wander down the **Boardwalk** to the Ferris wheel with a difference – 16 of the 24 carriages on **Deno's Wonder Wheel** swing to and fro as they go around. Afterwards, try some of the other rides – some are only suitable for toddlers, but there are several which are fun for older kids, teens and even adults. The **Luna Park Amusement Park** is a blast – it not only has thrill rides and family rides, it even has a few rides for little kids. If you're 137cm (54 inches) or taller, you'll be able to ride Coney Island's most famous old **roller coaster** – the Cyclone. If there's time, go to the **ballpark** (pg 17) and cheer the Brooklyn Cyclones on. Don't forget to eat one of **Nathan's Famous hot dogs** (pg 44) while you're there! Coney Island is at its best during the summer season, which runs from the last Monday in May to the first Monday in September. If you're in NYC between October and mid-April, save your visit for next time.

TAKE A FERRY TO LADY LIBERTY

Statue Cruises Tel: 1-877-523-9849
Visit the lady with the torch and cruise the harbor! If you just want to see the **Statue of Liberty** from afar, you can take the free **Staten Island Ferry** (pg 8) which will give you a great view as you sail past. If, however, you'd like to visit **Liberty Island** (where the statue is) or neighboring **Ellis Island** (which has a museum about the people who arrived to make a new home in the USA about a hundred years ago), go on a **Statue Cruise** from Battery Park, Manhattan, or from Liberty State Park, New Jersey. Book tickets in advance by calling the number above or online (*www.statuecruises.com*) to avoid the long lines. Don't bother going to Liberty

Island unless you want to climb up inside the Statue (you'll need to buy tickets in advance) because there isn't much else to do. Set off early if you want to visit both islands, and prepare to do lots of walking!

VISIT THE AMERICAN MUSEUM OF NATURAL HISTORY (AMNH)

Central Park W at 79th St, Manhattan
Tel: 1-212-769-5100

There are many fabulous museums in NYC, but the AMNH is one of the best. It's also one of the largest museums in the world. Although it has 46 permanent exhibition halls, it can only display a small portion of the objects in its collection at any given time, as it has more than 30 million specimens! When you arrive, grab a map and decide where you want to go – there is a lot to see! As well as the world-famous animal halls (with huge, realistic recreations of animals in their habitat), there are displays showing how our caveman ancestors lived, a hall full of fantastic dinosaur fossils, some massive gemstones and a room all about meteorites ('space rocks') – including the largest meteorite on display in the world! As if that weren't enough, there's the **Hayden Planetarium** (pg 34). When you're done, go outside and enjoy the park that the museum's on, or have a drink at one of the outdoor cafés that line the streets around the museum.

Sail the Harbor on the Staten Island Ferry – for free

From Whitehall Ferry Terminal, 4 South Street, Manhattan. Tel: 1-718-815-2628

This amazing ferry service runs all day and all night, every day – and is totally free! There's no guide to tell you about the sights, and during rush hour it can get crowded, but it's fine if you travel between 10am and 3pm. A one-way trip takes about half an hour – and you'll get a great view of **Lady Liberty**, **Brooklyn Bridge**, and **Governors Island** (pg 25). Many people do the round trip without touring **Staten Island**, but if you do want to stop and explore, you'll find a small zoo (pg 13), several museums (e.g. **Staten Island Children's Museum** – pg 35), a ballpark (home of the Staten Island Yankees), **Historic Richmond Town** – a historic village which has been turned into a museum – and sandy beaches. There are also several large areas of parkland in which you can kayak, hike, bike or enjoy a picnic.

Want to be the captain?
Rent a radio-controlled model boat in Central Park!
(See pg 22)

Ride Big Toot
**From North Cove Marina,
Battery Park City, Manhattan**

Every weekend, from May to October, Big Toot – a former US Navy launch – does several 50-minute tours around Liberty and Ellis Islands. Kids ride for free, while parents pay a reasonable fee. You can't reserve – it is first come, first served – but if the boat's full, you can go to the Floating Classroom in the marina and get a pass for a trip later in the day. Big Toot leaves North Cove in **Battery Park** at 9, 10 and 11am, then 1, 2, 3pm and 4pm. If it's very windy and the sea is rough, or if it's raining steadily, then Big Toot does not run. Unfortunately there's no way you can check if the service has been cancelled, so use your judgement!

The Beast Speedboat Tour
**From Pier 83,
West 42nd St & Twelfth Avenue, Manhattan
Tel: 1-212-563-3200**

Roar around the harbor in half an hour and see the sights! Part thrill ride, part sightseeing tour, the Beast Speedboat Tour is perfect for families who want a fun-filled ride (expect to get wet!), or for those in a hurry. In good weather, the tour runs hourly from noon to dusk, between May 1st and September 30th. All participants have to be over 40 inches/ 1m tall. If you are visiting off-season or prefer a more leisurely tour, the Circle Line Sightseeing company that runs the speedboat tour also runs a variety of more leisurely cruises. Call or check their website (*www.circleline42.com*) for details.

Relax in a Venetian Gondola

Loeb Boathouse, Central Park, East 72nd St & Park Drive North, Manhattan. Tel: 1-212-517-2233

Ride a gondola from Venice, Italy – in the middle of Manhattan! The boatman wears the same stripy shirt and straw hat as the gondoliers in Italy; and if you're lucky, he'll sing for you too! These half-hour rides are popular, so reserve by calling the number above.

Rowing and pedal boating

Feel like rowing? Hire a rowboat from the Loeb Boathouse in **Central Park** (contact details above). Rowboats and pedal boats are also available from the Lake Club in **Staten Island** (1150 Clove Road, Clove Lakes Park. Tel: 1-718-442-3600) or you can pedal a boat on the Kate Wollman Rink in **Brooklyn** (East Drive & Lincoln Road, Prospect Park. Tel: 1-718-282-7789). Only available during the warmer months – call for details.

Whiz across the ice

Sky Rink, Pier 61, Chelsea Piers, 23rd St & the Hudson River, Manhattan. Tel: 1-212-336-6100

You can ice-skate all year long at the **Chelsea Piers Sports Complex**, but during winter, there are lots of other places to try. From October to March, rent skates and whiz about in the open-air **Ice Rink at Rockefeller Center** (Fifth Avenue, between 49th & 50th St, Manhattan. Tel: 1-212-332-7654), or at these two rinks in Central Park, Manhattan: the **Wollman Rink** (near Central Park Zoo, Sixth Avenue & 59th St. Tel: 1-212-439-6900), or the less-crowded **Lasker Rink** (106th & 108th St. Tel: 1-917-492-3857).

... AND IN THE WATER

Jones Beach

Jones Beach State Park

It's a hassle to get to Jones Beach! You have to take the Long Island Rail Road (LIRR) from Penn Station in Manhattan to Freeport, then catch a bus. But fans claim it's the nicest beach in New York. If you'd rather

go to a closer beach, try Far Rockaway Beach or Long Beach – both are accessible on the LIRR – or the beach on Coney Island.

Splish Splash Water Park

2549 Splish Splash Drive, Calverton, Long Island
Tel: 1-631-727-3600
If your parents are renting a car, this water park is a fun destination – with thrilling slides, inner-tube shoots, wave pools and more. It gets crowded and rowdy during summer weekends, so try to get there before 9.30am. There are tons of rides for both adults and kids. On the scariest rides there are some height restrictions, but if you are over 48 inches/ 1.2m (about 8-9 years old), you should be able to go on most of them. For younger kids, there are 5 'kids-only' rides; you'll be able to go on most others with an adult. Swimming suits are essential and sunscreen is recommended. Open May to September.

Bronx Zoo

2300 Southern Boulevard, Bronx Park, Bronx
Tel: 1-718-220-5100

Bronx Zoo is the oldest zoo in the USA and it is HUGE, so find out when the feeding times of your favorite animals are, and plan your trip well! It has many sections. Some are outdoors – such as the African Plains exhibit, Tiger Mountain, and the Children's Zoo – while others are indoors, e.g. the warm and steamy JungleWorld, the Sea Bird Colony, or the Butterfly Garden. Visit lazy lions, hissing snakes, honking sea lions, and brightly colored frogs. And don't forget the strange animals from Madagascar and the majestic Congo Gorilla Forest. There are about 450 different species living in the zoo, so you'll be spoiled with options. If your feet get tired of all that walking, you can catch the Zoo Shuttle or take a ride on the monorail through the Asian Animals exhibit. The zoo is open year-round (except on major holidays), but some of the exhibits – such as the Children's Zoo and the monorail

ANIMALS

– are closed during the winter. It tends to be crowded on Wednesdays (when you can get in for free) and on the weekends, so if possible, go in the morning on a Monday or Tuesday!

Smaller zoos

Small zoos have fewer animals, but on the plus side: there's less walking involved; they're still big enough to give you an animal 'fix'; and you'll have enough time to go somewhere else that day. The best-known, is the zoo in **Central Park**, Manhattan (pgs 5, 22, 58), but if you are in the neighborhood, you may want to check out **Queens Zoo** (53-51, 111th St, Flushing, Queens. Tel: 1-718-271-5100), **Prospect Park Zoo** (450 Flatbush Ave, Brooklyn. Tel: 1-718-399-7339) or **Staten Island Zoo** (614 Broadway, Staten Island. Tel: 1-718-442-3100).

New York Aquarium
Surf Avenue & West 8th St, Coney Island, Brooklyn
Tel: 1-718-265-2663

Take a two or three-hour detour to visit this small but decent aquarium when you visit Coney Island (pg 6). The exhibits – especially the shark and ray tank – are interesting and the sea lion show is cute, though rather short. When you're done watching the live creatures on display, you can see a 4-D show, or go to the coastal display, where you can experience what tidal waves feel like to an ocean dweller. It's best to visit the aquarium on a good-weather day, as many of its attractions are outside. It is open all year from 10am. During the summer it stays open until 6pm/7pm (weekday/end), but it closes at 4.30pm during the winter.

Atlantis Marine World Aquarium
431 E Main St, Riverhead, Long Island
Tel: 1-631-208-9200

It's a long way from Manhattan, but if you're going to Long Island, you should consider visiting this aquarium. Apart from all the usual things you would expect at an aquarium, such as huge tanks full of colorful fish, they also have otters, sea lions, penguins, seals, sharks and rays. If you are brave enough (and old enough), you can have an interactive adventure – dip your hands into the Touch Tank, snorkel in a pool with fish and rays, float protected by a cage in the gigantic shark tank or get a kiss from a sea lion. There are some rides too, such as the submarine simulator, the viewing tower, as well as a playground with a climbing wall.

Queens County Farm Museum

73-50 Little Neck Parkway, Floral Park, Queens
Tel: 1-718-347-3276

They call it a museum but it is actually a historic farm that's been working non-stop since 1697! It's open every day, from 10am-5pm. You can get tours of the farmhouse and a hayride during the weekend, weather permitting. There are lots of farm animals to visit – don't forget to feed the friendly goats! Entry is free unless there is a special event, such as the Easter Egg Hunt or the County Fair. These special events are fun but tend to be extremely crowded.

HORSES

Ride like royalty

Ride a horse-drawn carriage through **Central Park**! You will find them standing in a line at Central Park South between Fifth & Sixth Avenues. Choose your favorite horse from those waiting, and go on a magical 20-minute tour of the park! Longer tours can be arranged but your parents will have to negotiate with the driver before you start. If it is very hot, very cold, or the park is closed, the horses will be sent home to rest.

Saddle up

There are a number of stables in New York – ask your hotel to recommend a good one. A stable that has a good reputation is the **Bronx Equestrian Center** (9 Shore Road, Bronx. Tel: 1-718-885-0551). You can have pony rides in the center itself, or go for a ride on a horse trail in Pelham Bay Park. Whether you're a beginner or an expert rider, you'll have fun!

ANIMALS

If you're in New York on the first Sunday in October, visit the lovely looking **Cathedral of St John the Divine** (1047 Amsterdam Avenue, Manhattan. Tel: 1-212-316-7490). On that day, to celebrate the feast day of St Francis of Assisi, the church holds a service with a difference – a blessing of animals! You'll see mostly cats and dogs, but the attendance of the occasional snake, bird of prey or even llama can add to the excitement!

EXPLORE &

See a Broadway musical

TKTS Discount Ticket Booth, Duffy Square, Broadway & 47th St, Times Square, Manhattan

The musicals staged on Broadway are usually spectacular – and a real treat to watch. Visit the website *www.broadway.com* or phone 1-800-276-23929 to check which shows are playing during your stay in New York (hint: if you're checking out the website, click on the 'Kid-Friendly' listing under 'Find A Show'). One of the best places to buy discounted genuine tickets is on the TKTS website (*www.entertainment-link.com/tkts.asp*) or at its Times Square booth (address above), where they are often half-price! You can only buy tickets for that day's performance at the booth – matinee tickets are sold from 10am-2pm, Wed & Sat, and 11am-3pm on Sunday. Evening tickets are sold Mon & Wed-Sat from 3pm-8pm, on Tuesday from 2pm-8pm, and on Sunday from 3pm.

Experience the New Victory Theater

209 West 42nd St, Manhattan
Tel: 1-646-223-3010

This theater is the only one in NYC that specializes in family-friendly shows. As well as performances (of plays, puppet theatre, dance and circus), it holds all sorts of interactive workshops for kids. Check online at *www.newvictory.org* for details!

If you're a teenager, and keen on the arts, check out www.highfivetix.org which sells tickets to hundreds of performances and events at only $5 each! Tickets to Broadway shows are rare, but there are tickets for a huge range of dance performances, plays, museums and films. Each teen can also buy an extra ticket for a parent or younger sibling. You'll need to take to the show some ID that shows your age.

EXPERIENCE

Go to a game!

Going to a **baseball game** (and eating a hot dog 'with everything') is an all-American thing to do! For the full experience, go see the New York Mets play in Citi Field in Flushing, Queens, or the New York Yankees play in Yankee Stadium in the Bronx. If you prefer a small stadium experience, go see a minor league team like the Staten Island Yankees or the Brooklyn Cyclones. Baseball season varies from year to year, but if you're in NYC between April and October, you should be able to catch a game. But if you're there during winter, go see a New York Rangers **ice-hockey game**, or a New York Knicks **basketball game** (both play in **Madison Square Garden**, Seventh Ave, 31st & 33rd St, Manhattan. Tel: 1-212-465-6741).

EXPLORE &

Whirl through the air at the Trapeze School

518 West 30th St, between Tenth & Eleventh Avenues, Manhattan. Tel: 1-212-242-8769

Anyone older than six can learn how to to perform on the flying trapeze! The **Trapeze School New York** has a few locations in NY: an indoor school which is used year round, as well as an outdoor 'rig' near the **Hudson River**, where you can soar freely in the open air, like a bird! They also hold occasional outdoor lessons on **Governors Island** (pg 25) during the summer. Call for more details.

Visit the Big Top!

If you love the magic of the circus, visit the **Ringling Bros. and Barnum & Bailey circus: Coney Island Illuscination** (Tel: 1-800-745-3000, *www.ringling.com*). It combines magic and animal acts (horses, elephants and lions) with acrobatics, clowns and heart-stopping stunts. The circus performs on Coney Island (21st St & Surf Avenue) for about three months starting in early June. Call for dates and to book. If you're in NY in the winter, try to catch the **Big Apple Circus**, which puts up its Big Top in Lincoln Center Plaza, Damrosch Park, Manhattan. The fun, music-packed performances are on from mid-October to January. Visit *www.bigapplecircus. org* for dates and tickets.

EXPERIENCE

Explore Chinatown

Wander through the busy streets of Chinatown in Manhattan, and sample some delicious food (dumplings, anyone? See pg 46) or buy an oriental souvenir. There is a Chinese department store called the **Pearl River Mart** (477 Broadway between Grand & Broome St. Tel: 1-212-431-4770) which is quite fun to look through for small, relatively inexpensive gifts. There's also the **Original Chinatown Ice Cream Factory** (65 Bayard St. Tel: 1-212-608-4170) where you can try the exotic (taro, chocolate pandan, black sesame or red bean) along with the more familiar, but equally delicious, flavors.

Join the midtown rush at Grand Central Terminal

87 E 42nd St, Manhattan

Even if you aren't planning to take the train anywhere, it's worth stopping at Grand Central. It is the largest train station in the world! While you are there, don't forget to look at the zodiac on the ceiling. Do you notice anything strange about it? Once you've done that, take your family to the dining area and find the **Oyster Bar**. The large entryway with the low-domed roof and ceramic arches is known as the Whispering Gallery. Stand in a corner diagonally opposite to your parents in the entryway, and whisper to each other while facing the walls. If it's not too crowded and noisy, you should be able to hear each other as clearly as if you were whispering into one another's ears!

See the city from the Empire State Building

350 Fifth Avenue, between 33rd & 34th St, Manhattan. Tel: 1-212-736-3100

The Empire State Building (ESB) is one of the best-known buildings in NYC and it's very popular with tourists. Because of this, you'll probably have to wait for a long time to get through the security line, the ticket line and the elevator line – unless you buy the (very expensive) express ticket, that guarantees you will be able to jump all three lines. You can, however,

EXPLORE &

skip the ticket line by booking online (*www.esbnyc.com*) or by getting a CityPASS (pg 4). There is an audio tour available that will tell you about the sights you can see from the 86th floor observatory (or the one on the 102nd floor – which you can visit for an additional fee). There's also an interactive ride called the **NY Skyride**; it allows you to 'fly' over NYC and see the sights. It's not all that exciting but entry to the ride includes express entry to the observatory, so you can cut down on waiting time. To go on the Skyride you have to be at least 36 inches/92cm tall.

Take the cable car to Roosevelt Island

Board at TramPlaza, Second Avenue, between 59th & 60th St, Manhattan. Tel: 1-212-832-4543

If you find yourself in midtown Manhattan, take a five-minute ride on an aerial tramway across the East River to **Roosevelt Island**. The gondolas soar high above the river, giving you awesome views of Queensboro Bridge and midtown Manhattan. There isn't much for tourists to do or see on the island, but you can take a stroll along the waterfront and admire the view, before taking the tram back to Manhattan again.

Go rock climbing at Brooklyn Boulders

575 Degraw St, Brooklyn
Tel: 1-347-834-9066

As long as you are three or older, you can visit New York's largest rock climbing studio and try to clamber up to the top of the kids' wall! You can rent all the equipment, and buy a day pass; but unless your parents are qualified to belay (work the safety ropes), you'll have to hire a member of staff as well, which can be quite expensive. Call for more details.

Zip along the Alley Pond Park Adventure Course Zipline

Winchester Boulevard, south of Grand Central Parkway, Queens. Tel: 1-718-217-4685

If you're aged 8 or above, you can participate in a free program held every Sunday from early May to late November, at New York's largest rope course! Whiz

EXPERIENCE

along a zipline or climb up a pole and throw yourself off (safely attached to a rope) during the thrilling two-hour itinerary. Because it's free, this activity is very popular, so make sure you get there early. From time to time the Center also runs a free overnight camping trip for families – with use of the rope course. Call the center for more details.

1 ROOSEVELT ISLAND

Central Park

Manhattan / See map on pg 58

There are so many things to do in Central Park, it's
hard to list them all! You can visit **the zoo** (pg 5),
enjoy a **horse-and-carriage ride** (pg 14), go **rowing** at
Loeb Boathouse (pg 10), **ice-skating** at the Wollman
and Lasker Rinks (pg 10) or even borrow rods and
bait and go **fishing** at the Charles A Dana Discovery
Center (Tel: 1-212-860-1370). In the summer you can
go **swimming** too, when the Lasker Rink turns into a
swimming pool (call for more details at 1-212-534-7639).

You can also **rent bikes** and helmets from April to
November at the Loeb Boathouse (call 1-212-517-2233
for details). If you'd like a **guided tour** along some of
the 47 miles/ 75km of paths, contact the Bike and Roll
Company (Tel: 1-212-260-0400). Their guides will ride
along with you to the major attractions of the park and
tell you lots of interesting facts too!

There are also **21 playgrounds**, a **carousel**, a **pond**
(called Conservatory Water) where you can pilot **radio-
controlled model boats** (call 1-917-522-0054 for boat
rentals – closed during winter), and **sculptures** which
you are encouraged to climb on (our favorite is the
Alice in Wonderland one).

If you'd like to join the thousands of in-line skaters
who whiz around the park, you can rent **in-line skates**
at Blades West (156 West 72nd St, between Columbus
Avenue & Broadway. Tel: 1-212-787-3911). The Park
Drives and the Bandshell are good places to skate.

When you're tired from all that physical activity, check out the **Chess & Checkers House** – you can borrow chess and checker pieces and have a relaxing game at the chess tables outside. Occasionally they also run holiday craft classes (call 1-212-794-4064 for details).

If you're reading this before you go, another cool thing you can do is to download the map and **family audio tour** from *www.centralpark.com/guide/tours/walking/ self-guided/download-audio.html* onto your MP3 player (e.g. iPod). Don't worry if you didn't do this – you can still get an audio tour of sorts via a mobile phone. Dial the phone number along with the location number you find on the green Central Park Conservancy signs dotted around the park. You'll be able to listen to a variety of celebrities tell you a bit about the area you are in! Some talk about why that particular spot is special to them, others talk about the location itself.

During the summer there are often **open-air performances** in the park too – poetry, Shakespearean plays, storytelling, orchestral performances and rock concerts. Ask your hotel what's on!

The High Line

Gansevoort St (Meatpacking District) to 34th St (not yet complete), between Tenth & Eleventh Avenues
This amazing park is built on disused freight-train tracks, high above the streets of west Manhattan. Section 1 opened in 2009, and Section 2 in Spring 2011. It is not known at the time of printing when the last section (to 34th St) will open. This long narrow park is

a lovely place for a stroll. There are lawns, seats, and aerial walkways that skim the tops of the trees. Access staircases (and some elevators) are located every couple of blocks along the length of the park.

Botanical Gardens

200th St and Kazimiroff Boulevard, Bronx
Tel: 1-718-817-8700
The NY Botanical Gardens isn't only about flowers and plants, though the flora has been carefully chosen to keep the gardens alight with color all year round. There's also the **Everett Children's Adventure Garden** (for kids aged 2-12), which includes mazes, floral sculptures and an indoor laboratory where you can do experiments! One of the highlights of the year is the annual **Christmas Train Show** exhibition – watch a miniature train wind around a huge glass house, in which over 140 of NYC's most famous tourist sights have been recreated using dried plants. Once you've seen that, go and visit the annual gingerbread house exhibition, drink hot chocolate and get into a wintery mood! Open Tue-Sun.

Hudson River Park

This park runs from north to south on Manhattan's western waterfront. The park connects a number of piers. Many of the piers are open to the public and contain a variety of features, such as the playgrounds with **interactive water areas** (great for cooling

off in, during the hot summer months) at pier 51. There are free kayaking sessions (on piers 96 and 40 during weekends and holidays from May-October) as well as kayaking lessons (on pier 66 - for a fee), a carousel on pier 62 (runs on weekends), and **Chelsea Piers** – from 59 to 61. Chelsea Piers is a sports complex where you can **ice skate** and play ten-pin **bowling** among other things. If you're aged between 5-15, you can try your hand at **fishing** too – join the free fishing lessons (no equipment required) held at the weekend during summer/ fall on pier 84 (call 1-212-627-2020). There's also an interactive science-themed water play area for kids and adults on pier 84.

Governors Island

Governors Island is less than 10 minutes away on the free ferry from the Battery Maritime Building, 10 South St, Manhattan. During the summer season you can take part in lots of **free activities** there. These include kayaking, **kite flying** (you even get a free kite), **fishing trips**, performances, art events (free **workshops** for kids!) and even free **bike rentals**. In past years, visitors have also been able to participate in events such as trapeze and unicycle classes, barbecues, concerts and much more. The only problem? It's open to visitors only Fri-Sun, from early June to the start of October.

IT'S RAINING,

New York is full of exciting stuff to do, whether the sun is shining or not! On wet, gray days, check out the amazing museums (pg 30). Or, blow off steam by rock climbing at Brooklyn Boulders (pg 20), swinging through the air at Trapeze School (pg 18), or trying one of the suggestions below:

New York Hall of Science

47-01, 111th St, Flushing Meadows Corona Park, Queens. Tel: 1-718-699-0005

You don't need to be a science nerd to enjoy the interactive displays – they are fabulous for anyone, from tots to grandparents! There is a multi-sensory preschool play area for the youngest visitors, as well as thought-provoking, squeal-inducing interactive displays for older kids (and adults). These displays explore all kinds of subjects, from microbes to space travel to the science of sports. If there's any time left, **Queens Zoo** and a **carousel** are located nearby.

Sony Wonder Technology Lab

Sony Plaza, 56th St & Madison Avenue, Manhattan. Tel: 1-212-833-8100 (automated line; speak to the group coordinator to reserve your tickets)

The SWTL is a four-story exhibition space in Manhattan, stuffed full of fascinating and interactive technological displays (how movies are made, how robots work, etc.) for all ages … And it's absolutely free. It's no wonder the SWTL is so popular! To reserve an entry ticket, call the number above at least seven days before you want to visit. If you haven't been able to reserve, you might be able to nab a same day entry ticket, but get there before they go on sale, as numbers are limited. The tickets are sold from 10am Tues-Sat and from

IT'S POURING

12pm on Sunday. The SWTL also screens animations once or twice a week, and for a small fee, visitors can also take part in various workshops (e.g. learn how to make your own animation or experiment with nano-technology). Call for more information on what's on. Closed on Mondays and major holidays.

Madame Tussauds

234 West 42nd St, Times Square, Manhattan
Tel: 1-800-246-8872

As with the London Madame Tussauds, you'll enjoy this attraction if you know lots of actors, musicians and famous people... but your younger brother or sister might get bored. Once you have had your photo taken with the President, Elvis, or even Edward the vampire from the *Twilight* series, you can go to watch a 4-D film or frighten your socks off in the interactive scary area, where live actors jump out when you least expect them (not recommended for younger kids). Open daily from 10am.

Ripley's Believe It or Not

234 West 42nd St, Times Square
Tel: 1-212-398-3133

Some people love the oddities in Ripley's, while others just find them gross – only you know which camp you're in! This rather expensive attraction, a neighbor of Madame Tussauds, is not suitable for young kids, or for those of a sensitive nature.

Catch a flick

There are zillions of cinemas all over New York and the easiest way to find the nearest one is to ask at your hotel. However, chances are, whichever mainstream movie you want to see, you'll find it at the mega-sized AMC Empire 25 in Times Square (234 42nd St, between 7th & 8th Avenues, Manhattan. Tel: 1-888-262-4386) which has 25 screens! If you're looking for a stunning documentary, try the huge IMAX screen at the AMNH (see pg 7/ Central Park W at 79th St, Manhattan Tel: 1-212-769-5200).

IT'S RAINING,

Animazing Gallery

Corner of Greene & Broome St, Manhattan
Tel: 1-800-303-4848

Ok, we know that kids and art galleries don't always
go hand in hand, but this gallery in SoHo is different.
It specializes in cool animation and illustration art –
everything from Charlie Brown to Spiderman to picture
books! Call them to find out what they're exhibiting
while you're in town.

Chelsea Piers Sports Complex

Chelsea Piers, 23rd St & Hudson River, Manhattan
Field House: pier 62. Tel: 1-212-336-6500
300 NY Alley: piers 59 &60. Tel: 1-212-835-2695
Sky Rink: pier 61. Tel: 1-212-336-6100

If you're feeling sporty, you'll have lots of options
at Chelsea Piers. At the Field House you can play
baseball, do some **gymnastics** and **rock climb**. It also
has a **Toddler Adventure Center**, which tots aged 6
months to 4 years will love. Not far away, between
piers 59 & 60 there is the 300 New York Alley where you
can **bowl**, or you can go do some **ice-skating** all
year round at Sky Rink (pg 10).

Bowlmor Lanes – ten-pin bowling

Union Square Bowlmor: 110 University Place,
12 & 13th St, Manhattan. Tel: 1-212-255-8188
Times Square Bowlmor: 222 West 44th St,
7th & 8th St, Manhattan. Tel: 1-212-680-0012

The newest Bowlmor in **Times Square** has six NYC-
themed rooms where you can bowl. We like the sound
of the Chinatown room, where a gong is rung every
time you get a strike! It isn't cheap but if you get
hungry, they'll deliver food right to your lane. The
seventh themed room is the Coney Island Room which
has a carnival theme and games.

You can, of course, also go bowling at the Bowlmor in
Union Square, but that's not all. Above the lanes is a
massive carnival-themed space, which is innocent and
fun during the day but at night turns into a nightclub.

IT'S POURING

During the day, both Bowlmor locations are fine for families (they have light balls and bumpers to make bowling easier for kids) but become rowdy, adult-only places after dark – so make sure you go there early, and leave before the evening.

New York has tons of great museums! We already covered two places devoted to the sciences on pg 26: New York Hall of Science and Sony Wonder Technology Lab, as well as the American Museum of Natural History (pg 7). Here are a few more suggestions:

Museum of Modern Art (MoMA)

11 West 53rd St, between Fifth & Sixth Avenues, Manhattan. Tel: 1-212-708-9400

Visit MoMA, one of the most famous art museums in the world – and see some amazing masterpieces in person! To get the most out of your visit, grab a free audio guide (suitable for kids aged 5 and up), get a family activity guide, or join a family gallery talk (available on weekends). The museum also shows films suitable for kids, boasts an interactive 'art space' for families and also hosts free drop-in workshops, pizza nights and artist talks for teens. Call for more details.

American Museum of the Moving Image

35th Avenue at 37th St, Astoria, Queens Tel: 1-718-777-6888

If you'd like to find out more about the history and technology behind movies, videos and TV, this museum is for you. Not only does it have family-friendly interactive exhibits and an arcade of classic video games (such as Pac-Man), the museum also holds occasional screenings of family movies and workshops for kids (aged 6-12) and teens, suitable for budding movie directors and animators alike!

Metropolitan Museum of Art

1000 Fifth Avenue, at 82nd St, Manhattan Tel: 1-212-535-7710

This is no ordinary art museum – "the Met" (as it's called) houses art from all over the world, spanning 5,000 years! The collection includes varied items such

as paintings, armor, musical instruments, glassware and sculptures – including massive sculptures, mummies and even a 2,000-year-old stone temple building from Ancient Egypt! We recommend you get a family audio guide (best for kids aged 6-12, though interesting for those who are older too!) and a free family map before you start exploring. It will help you plan your visit, and it's fun to learn interesting snippets of information as you wander around. There are also many different programs for visitors aged 5-18 such as art workshops, talks, tours and drawing sessions. Call or visit the information counter to find out what's on when you visit.

Intrepid Sea, Air & Space Museum

Pier 86, W 46th St & Twelfth Avenue, Manhattan
Tel: 1-212-245-0072

If you like big powerful vehicles, you'll be in heaven at this midtown museum; but there's plenty here to interest everyone in your family! Not only do you get to see the inner workings of a battleship (the USS Intrepid), you can also see what living on a submarine (the USS Growler) would have been like. Experience supersonic thrust on the G Force Encounter Simulator (height requirement is 48 inches/ 1.2m), then take a stroll along the aisle of the supersonic Concorde, before trying the 4-D Motion Ride Theater and the FX Flight Simulator (you must be 38 inches / 96 cm or taller for both these rides). When you've done all that, calm your nerves by exploring the Exploreum Hall – it is full of interesting interactive displays and tons of fascinating facts about being in space, at sea, or flying through the air. Audio tours for both kids and adults – with interesting stories from famous figures such as astronaut Scott Carpenter – are also available. Closed on Mondays during winter, and on major holidays.

Children's Museum of the Arts

182 Lafayette St, between Broome & Grand St, Manhattan. Tel: 1-212-274-0986

This SoHo museum houses quirky exhibitions of art designed to interest everyone in the family, and also has a collection of over 2,000 pieces of art made by young people from all over the world. Every exhibition is designed to appeal to kids aged 1-12, as are the daily free art and drama workshops; the programs allow you to explore your artistic muse, or dress up and strut the stage. Open Wed-Sun from 12pm.

NYC Fire Museum

278 Spring St, Manhattan
Tel: 1-212-691-1303

Located in SoHo in a renovated fire station built more than 100 years ago, this museum is full of history. You can see how fire-fighting equipment has improved since the 1790s! The museum is fairly small, but it's worth a

quick visit if you are passing by. Sadly, the guided tours that the museum operates are only open to private bookings, for groups of 20 or more. Open Tuesday to Sunday from 10am.

NYC Police Museum

**100 Old Slip, South Street Seaport, Manhattan
Tel: 1-212-480-3100**

This is another small museum which is worth visiting if you're interested in the police, or in the area. There is an interactive play area for kids 3-10. Open Mon-Sat from 10am-5pm, and Sun from 12pm-5pm.

NYC Transit Museum

Corner of Boerum Place & Schermerhorn St, Brooklyn Heights. Tel: 1-718-694-1792/1600

Set in a real (disused) subway station, this museum is fun to visit and will excite train fans, who not only can look at displayed trains, but board them too! Every weekend, the museum runs family programs generally suitable for kids aged 4 and above. Call for more details for what's on. If Brooklyn is too far to travel to, there is a small branch of the Transit Museum at Grand Central Terminal in Manhattan (pg 19). Closed on Mondays and major holidays.

Lower East Side Tenement Museum

97 & 108 Orchard St, Manhattan
Tel: 1-212-982-8420

This museum in the Lower East Side is an odd one, as you can't wander around and explore. Instead, you must join a tour to visit the apartments in the tenement block. On the tour, you'll learn what life was like for an immigrant about 100 years ago. Suitable for older kids and their parents (some tours are for ages 8+, while others are for 12+), the tours are led by enthusiastic and knowledgeable guides who bring history alive. Check out the website (*www.tenement.org/tours.php*) to see what tours are available. Tours start at 108 Orchard St.

Hayden Planetarium & the Rose Center for Earth & Space

West 81st St, Manhattan. Tel: 1-212-769-5100

The Hayden Planetarium in the Upper West Side is part of the **American Museum of Natural History** (AMNH, pg 7) and is accessible from the main museum entrance too. But if you especially love learning about space and **space exploration**, consider doing a special visit to the Rose Center alone (there is too much other stuff to see in the AMNH). As well as informative displays on planets and the universe, visitors can enjoy a virtual reality show in the **Space Theater** (try to sit near the back) and a re-creation of the beginnings of the universe in the Big Bang Theater. Open 10am-5.45pm.

Solomon R. Guggenheim Museum

1071 Fifth Avenue, Manhattan
Tel: 1-212-423-3500

The Guggenheim Museum (in the Upper East Side) is housed in a building which is almost as fascinating as the fantastic modern art collection within it. From the outside, you can see that the building is built in a spiral – and you'll understand why when you get inside – the art is arranged on the walls of a gallery that spirals up to the dome roof. The museum runs tours, workshops and interactive projects for families most Sundays. Call for more details.

FOR YOUNGER BROTHERS & SISTERS

There are several **children's museums** in or around
New York City – one in **Manhattan** (Tisch Bldg, 212
West 83rd St, Manhattan. Tel: 1-212-721-1223), one in
Staten Island (Snug Harbor Cultural Center, 1000
Richmond Terrace, Staten Island. Tel: 1-718-273-2060),
one in **New Jersey** (599 Valley Health Plaza, Paramus,
NJ. Tel: 1-201-262-5151) and one in **Brooklyn**. The
Brooklyn Children's Museum is considered the most
interesting (145 Brooklyn Avenue at St Marks
Avenue, Brooklyn. Tel: 1-718-735-4400. Open
Tues-Sun, 10am-5pm) . Although these
museums say they are suitable for kids
aged 2-12, little tots will enjoy
them the most.

FAO Schwarz

767 Fifth Avenue at 58th St, Manhattan
Tel: 1-212-644-9400

This is one of the most famous toy stores in the world, and when you walk in, you'll know why. Play with the toys on display – or watch the many demonstrations that take place continuously all over the shop. One of the most popular sights in the store is the 21-foot-long (6.7m) walk-on 'piano'. Dance on the keyboard and see if you can play a tune, or watch professional dancers do so! You can also go on a virtual ride, shake hands with a toy soldier, or pat the huge stuffed elephants and giraffes. If you need even more of a buzz, there's a candy shop called FAO Schweetz, which sells a massive range of candy. Open Monday-Saturday from 10am, and on Sunday from 11am.

u DROP

Books of Wonder

18 W 18th St, Manhattan. Tel: 1-212-989-3270

If you're looking for a good read, head to the Flatiron district to NY's oldest and largest independent children's bookshop. There are many departments stocking all kinds of books; so whether you are looking for a picture book, hilarious middle-grade book or an edgy young-adult novel, you should find it here. After you've made your purchase, have a yummy sweet treat at the **Cupcake Café** which is right inside the shop! Open 10am-7pm, and on Sunday 11am-6pm.

Tannen's Magic

Suite 608, 45 W 34th St, Manhattan
Tel: 1-212-929-4500

Abracadabra! Behold, a magic shop! Amateur magicians will find all sorts of nifty tricks to buy in this store. If you need some help in actually performing them, you can even book some lessons. The company recommends private lessons for those aged 8 and over, though teens can join a group lesson. If you're around at the right time, there are also occasional workshops for beginner magicians aged 7-9, and for those aged 10-17. Call the shop for more details.

Nintendo World

10 Rockefeller Plaza, Manhattan
Tel: 1-646-459-0800

This massive store in midtown will feel like paradise to anyone who likes computer games! Apart from stocking almost everything Nintendo that you might think of, the shop has several 'stations' where fans can try out the latest games on the DS and Wii. Open Mon-Thur 9am-8pm, on Saturday 9am-9pm, on Sunday 11am-6pm.

Paragon Sports

867 Broadway, Manhattan
Tel: 1-212-255-8889

If you're a sports fanatic, you'll love Paragon Sports, which boasts that it stocks 50,000 items in its store!

Brooklyn Superhero Supply Company

372 Fifth Avenue, Brooklyn
Tel: 1-718-499-9884

Where's a superhero to go when he needs de-villainizing 'justice spray' or a superhero cape? Why, to the Superhero Supply Company, of course! This shop stocks tons of fun products, disguises, costumes (in kids and adult sizes) and potions (like the one for invisibility). There's even a machine in the shop where you can test out capes! However, *ahem*, there is a small catch: the sprays and lotions don't work in real life, and most of the stuff in the shop wouldn't help if you were faced with a real supervillain. But hey, they make fun gifts, and you can always buy something to put on your bedroom shelf to make your visitors wonder if you *really* have x-ray vision. Best of all, the money raised in the store is given to a charity that teaches writing skills to kids aged 6-18, so you can spend knowing that your money is being put to good use.

Dylan's Candy Bar & Café

1011 Third Avenue at 60th St, Manhattan
Tel: 1-646-735-0078

You'll probably have to promise your mom that you won't buy or eat everything in sight, but it'll be hard to keep that promise once you enter this three-story candy heaven! Once you've tried the samples, made your choice and filled your pick-n-mix bags, have your picture taken with Chocolate, the mascot bunny.

u DROP

Economy Candy
108 Rivington St, Manhattan
Tel: 1-212-254-1531
An old-fashioned candy store in the Lower East Side that sells everything you could wish for: chocolates, candy, nuts and even dried fruit. It's a sweet paradise!

Crewcuts
1190 Madison Avenue, between 87th & 88th St, Manhattan
Tel: 1-212-348-9803
This huge shop in the Upper East Side is an experience. Check out the junior J. Crew fashions (for boys and girls aged 2-10, who want to look like their trendy older siblings or parents!), and enjoy the fun art installations displayed If clothes are not your they also have a small selection of books and toys on sale.

Forbidden Planet
840 Broadway, Manhattan
Tel: 1-212-473-1576
This Union Square shop is *geektastic!* It's full of comics, manga and sci-fi, as well as games, books, t-shirts and toys (everything from trading cards to Transformers).

New York Costumes

Entrances at 104 Fourth Avenue & 808 Broadway, Manhattan. Tel: 1-212-673-4546

In the market for a costume, a witch's broomstick or maybe a wig? If you couldn't find it at the Brooklyn Superhero Supply Company, try this place in Greenwich Village instead. They stock goods for 'adults, children, and everyone in between'!

Boomerang Toys

119 W Broadway, Manhattan
Tel: 1-212-226-7650

Boomerang Toys in Tribeca specializes in toys for tots and pre-schoolers. It also has a stock of board games, building systems and science kits for older kids. There's also another branch in Manhattan, in the World Financial Center, 222 Liberty Street.

u DROP

McNally Jackson Bookshop

52 Prince St, Lafayette & Mulberry, Manhattan
Tel: 1-212-274-1160

This SoHo bookstore will keep the whole family happy as they have a huge selection of books from picture books to young-adult reads and adult books. There is a **café** within the store, and on Fridays and Saturdays there is often a storytime session for babies and kids under 7. Call for more details.

Barnes & Noble

Many locations including several in Manhattan:
Union Square, 33 East 17th St. Tel: 1-212-253-0810
555 Fifth Avenue. Tel: 1-212-697-3048
82nd & Broadway. Tel: 1-212-362-8835
97 Warren St, Tribeca. Tel: 1-212-587-5389

B&N is the largest chain of bookstores in the USA. You'll find their huge stores all over NYC! In addition to books, they also stock toys, games, DVDs and CDS. Several branches run regular **storytelling** sessions for children. Please call for details.

Strand Book Store

828 Broadway by 12th St, Manhattan
Tel: 1-212-473-1452

This huge bookstore in Greenwich Village has been open since 1927! They have a great stock of new, used and antique books in their store. They also run a kiosk in Central Park.

Macy's Department Store

Herald Square, between 34th & 35th on Broadway, Manhattan (entrances also on 34th St and Seventh Avenue). Tel: 1-212-695-4400

Macy's is known as the biggest department store in the world – and boy is there a lot to see and buy in it! There are 10 floors to wander about on, and it's easy to get lost, so make sure you pick up a map of the store as you enter. Before you go, check out *www.visitmacysusa.com/visitors/savings.cfm* and download discount vouchers. Overseas visitors may have to take their passports to claim the 10% discount card.

FOOD, GLORI

New York is full of restaurants –
from cheap and cheerful, to gourmet!
Below is a list of quirky, casual places
recommended by NYC foodies!

COMFORT FOOD & ALL-AMERICAN DINING

The Meatball Shop

**84 Stanton St, between Allen &
Orchard St, Manhattan
Tel: 1-212-982-8895**

Get here early because you can't
reserve a table, and this Lower
East Side place is popular!
The food is simple: you
choose a 'meatball' type
(beef, spicy pork, chicken,
vegetarian or the special)
plus a sauce (spicy meat,
tomato, mushroom, pesto,
the 'special sauce' or creamy
cheese) and whether you
want all of that served as a
sandwich, on risotto, pasta
or mashed potatoes! If you're
feeling healthy, there's lots of
vegetable side dishes, from salad, to
broccoli, to roast veggies. Yum!

S'Mac

**345 East 12th St, Manhattan
Tel: 1-212-358-7912**

S'Mac (pronounced *smack*) is short for 'Sarita's
macaroni and cheese' – and the name says it all! But
this East Village temple to affordable comfort-food
doesn't only serve standard mac & cheese (though it is
yummy!). It has 12 different and delicious variations,
including a low-calorie version, one with meat, plus
French, Italian and even Indian versions. If you can't

OUS FOOD

decide, get the sampler – you get small portions of six varieties. If, on the other hand, none of the menu options appeal to you, you can even build your own.

EJ's Luncheonette

Upper West Side: 447 Amsterdam Avenue & W 82nd St. Tel: 1-212-873-3444
Upper East Side: 1271 Third Avenue, between 73rd & 74th St. Tel: 1-212-472-0600

Stop by for a scrumptious brunch at this family-friendly retro diner! New Yorkers seem to prefer the Upper West Side branch, but both serve traditional diner food – breakfast specialities are particularly recommended. You can't book a table, so be prepared to wait if you go at peak times.

Pintaile's Pizza

Upper East Side branches:
1573 York Avenue, E 84th St.
Tel: 1-212- 396-3479
26 E 91st St (Fifth & Madison)
Tel: 1-212-722-1967

The specialty of the house is crisp, paper-thin crust pizza – just like they serve in Italy! Creative toppings and yummy salads round out the menu.

Motorino Pizza

Two branches:
East Village: 349 East 12th St at Second Avenue, Manhattan. Tel: 1-212-777-2644
Brooklyn: 319 Graham Avenue, Devoe St, Brooklyn Tel: 1-718-599-8899

Motorino was voted the best pizza in New York City by the *New York Times* food critic! This pizza joint serves yummy pizza with chewy crust and a host of delicious toppings – including seasonal favorites. For dessert, if you still have room, try the bombolini – which are like little Italian jelly donuts – they are recommended!

FOOD, GLORI

Shake Shack

Several locations in Manhattan including –
Madison Square Park: SE corner, near Madison
Avenue & E 23rd St. Tel: 1-212-889-6600
Theatre District: 691 8th Avenue, corner of Eighth
Avenue & 44th St. Tel: 1-646-435-0135

Shake Shack started as a hot dog stand, and its hot
dogs still have a good reputation, but most people go
for the burgers, fries and frozen-custard shakes. Expect
to wait if you go at peak times! At the original Madison
Square Park location, you can choose to sit in the Shake
Shack outdoor dining area, or on one of the shady park
benches nearby to enjoy your food.

Nathan's Famous

Several locations including –
Manhattan: 1286 Broadway. Tel: 1-212-630-0315
Coney Island: 1310 Surf Avenue, Boardwalk, Coney
Island, Brooklyn. Tel: 1-718-946-2705

Nathan's is famous for their hot dogs (they even host an
annual hot dog eating contest) which they serve plain
or with a variety of toppings. They also serve crinkle-
cut fries, burgers, fried chicken and all sorts of other
unhealthy but yummy treats.

BAGELS

New Yorkers love their bagels – chewy donut-shaped
bread, which is delicious hot out of the oven and eaten
with cream cheese and smoked salmon! You can buy
bagels almost anywhere – but here are some of the best
places to go to get your bagel fix: **Ess-a-Bagel** (two
locations in Manhattan: 359 First Avenue, at 21st St; and
831 Third Avenue, between 51st & 52nd St) which sells
bagels, salads, pastries, muffins and cakes; **Murray's
Bagels** (two locations in Manhattan: 500 Sixth Avenue,
between 12th & 13th St, Greenwich Village; and 242
Eighth Avenue, between 22nd & 23rd Streets); and
Bagel Hole (400 Seventh Avenue, between 12th & 13th
St, Park Slope, Brooklyn).

OUS FOOD

Momofuku Noodle Bar

**171 First Avenue, between 10th & 11th St, Manhattan
Tel: 1-212-777-7773**

If you are in the East Village, slurp down a delicious hot bowl of noodles or have some Japanese-inspired dishes at this casual noodle bar. No reservations, so try to get there early so you don't have to wait! Open for lunch 12pm-4pm, and for dinner from 5.30pm.

Taïm

222 Waverly Pl, between Perry & W 11th St, Manhattan. Tel: 1-212-691-6101

If you're vegetarian, or even if you're not, you'll enjoy the falafel sandwiches served at this tiny hole-in-the-wall restaurant. Falafel (crunchy, fried chickpea patties) are delicious smothered in lemony sesame sauce!

Prosperity Dumpling

46 Eldridge St, Chinatown, Manhattan
Tel: 1-212-343-0683

Don't come expecting a lovely atmosphere and gourmet food, but if you want to have a quick dish of cheap and cheerful dumplings or yummy sesame pancakes, you'll enjoy this Chinatown fave!

Shun Lee Café

43 W 65th St, Manhattan
Tel: 1-212-769-8895

If you want a proper, fancy Chinese meal, go to the Shun Lee Restaurant next door. But if you're looking for delicious dim sum dumplings and buns, served in the traditional way out of carts pushed around by the waiters, then the Café is your place. Reservations are recommended. Open for dinner all week, but for lunch only Sat-Sun from 11.30am-2.30pm.

SWEET TREATS

Sweetiepie

19 Greenwich Avenue, between Christopher &
W 10th St, Manhattan. Tel: 1-212-337-3333

Girls will love the princess-pink interior of this West Village restaurant. There are savory dishes on the menu, but from what we hear, dessert is the best part! Go for afternoon tea – if you're lucky, you'll be able to sit at the table inside the golden birdcage!

Magnolia Bakery

West Village: 401 Bleecker St. Tel: 1-212-462-2572
200 Columbus Avenue. Tel: 1-212-724-8101
Rockefeller Center. Tel: 1-212-767-1123
Grand Central Terminal. Tel: 1-212-682-3588

This bakery is most famous for its cupcakes but they also make yummy cakes, bars, cookies and pies. Their website looks delicious, too: *www.magnoliabakery.com*. The West Village location is the flagship store and is considered a NYC landmark!

ChikaLicious Dessert Bar
**203 E 10th St, near Second Avenue, Manhattan
Tel: 1-212-995-9511**
This tiny dessert bar in the East Village is often crowded as people flock there to satisfy their sweet tooth, so be prepared to wait. Open Thur-Sun 3pm-late.

Original Chinatown Ice-Cream Factory
Yummy Asian-inspired flavors as well as all the usual favorites (pg 19).

Cupcake Café
Buy a good book at **Books of Wonder** (pg 37) and then settle into the in-store café for some quiet reading time with a hot drink and a delicious cupcake.

FOOD, GLORI

Christopher Norman Chocolates
60 New St, Manhattan
Tel: 1-212-402-1243
OK, so this is a store not a restaurant – but they *will* make you a cup of cocoa to sip as you watch delicious chocolates being made, and decide what you want from the tempting display! Heaven for chocoholics.

Serendipity 3
225 East 60th St, Manhattan
Tel: 1-212-838-3531
Although you can get a good lunch or dinner here, most people come for the desserts, especially the Frozen Hot Chocolate! You can't reserve a table for desserts, so go early in the afternoon, on a weekday, to beat the crowds.

Gian & Piero Bakery
44-19 30th Avenue, Astoria, Queens
Tel: 1-718-274-8959
If you're visiting the Museum of the Moving Image (pg 30), stop by at this Italian bakery and try their 'amazing' pastries. The cannolis are described as fantastic!

SODA PIZZA CUPCAKES

OUS FOOD

Jiannetto's Pizza Truck

Grab a slice of pizza from 10am-3pm, on weekdays. The trucks are parked on 47th St, between Park & Madison Avenues (Tel: 1-917-287-7241); and also at the NE corner of Front St & Wall St (Tel: 1-917-753-0819).

Biriyani Cart

Handmade gourmet Indian food – to take away! Get a spicy and delicious snack. The cart is parked at 46th St & Sixth Avenue. Tel: 1-917-628-3269.

Calexico

Want delicious Mexican food? Try this cart, parked in SoHo at Wooster St, near Prince St. Tel: 1-917-674-1869.

Treats Truck

Get a delicious sweet treat – sink your teeth into a cookie or a brownie … mmm! The Treats Truck travels to different areas of Manhattan. Call 1-212-691-5226 to find out where they are, or check their schedule at *www.treatstruck.com*.

Food trucks are all the rage in NYC. If you see one with a long line of people waiting to be served, that usually means the food's great — go have a taste!

FAST FACTS

- New York City is located on the east coast of the USA. Its nickname is the 'Big Apple', and it has a reputation as 'the city that never sleeps'! Although Washington DC is the capital, NYC is the largest city in the USA, with more than 8 million residents.

- New York used to be part of 'New Netherland' – a Dutch colonial settlement. It was known as 'New Amsterdam' until 1674, when, after many years of fighting, the English took control of the area and renamed it 'New York'.

- From the 1600s to about 1950, millions of immigrants sailed into New York Harbor to start a new life in America. You can learn about the 12 million people who entered the US via Ellis Island – an immigration center between 1892 to 1954 – at the immigration museum there.

- The currency of the USA is the US dollar, which is divided into cents. A 1-cent coin is sometimes called a 'penny', a 5-cent coin is known as a 'nickel', a 10-cent coin is known as a 'dime', and a 25-cent coin is a 'quarter'.

- New York enjoys four seasons. In the summer, it can be steamy and hot, with temperatures rising above 86°F (30°C) in July and August. Winters are cold! Temperatures drop to an average of 26°F (-3°C) in January and February.

HOLIDAYS

Some attractions may be closed during the following holidays, so check before you go!

January 1st: New Year's Day

Third Monday in January: Martin Luther King Jr. Day

Third Monday in February: Presidents' Day

Last Monday in May: Memorial Day

July 4th: Independence Day

First Monday in September: Labor Day

Second Monday in October: Columbus Day

November 11th: Veterans Day

Fourth Thursday in November: Thanksgiving Day

December 25th: Christmas Day

NYC TRAVEL TIPS

- New York City is made up of five boroughs: Manhattan, Brooklyn, the Bronx, Queens and Staten Island.

- New York, like many major cities, suffers from heavy traffic, and it is often quicker and easier to walk – so make sure you pack comfortable shoes!

- It's easy to find your way around central Manhattan because many of the streets are arranged in a grid. As a general rule of thumb, the avenues run vertically along the length of Manhattan – First Avenue is on the eastern edge, while Twelfth Avenue runs along the western edge. The streets are narrower and run at right angles to the avenues, and they increase in number the farther north you go. Confusingly, between Third and Fifth Avenue, there is no 'Fourth Avenue' but you'll find three other avenues called (from east to west) Lexington, Park and Madison Avenue! Sixth Avenue is sometimes known as Avenue of the Americas.

- If you intend to use the Metro or buses a lot, your parents might want to buy a MetroCard – which gives you unlimited rides. These are available as a 1-day, 7-day or two-week pass from the MetroCard Vending Machines in subway stations. Up to 3 children (less than 44 inches/ 112 cm tall) can ride free with a fare-paying adult, so you may not need to buy passes for the whole family.

SPEAK THE LINGO

Here are some terms that might help you blend in with the natives!

Buck: Dollar – i.e. the game cost twenty bucks! (More money terms on pg 50)

Going crosstown: Travel from the west side of Manhattan to the east, or vice versa (i.e. from First Avenue to Tenth Avenue)

Stand on line: Stand in line/queue

Crosswalk: A pedestrian crossing

Bodega: A corner shop

Hero sandwich: Also known as a 'sub' – it is a long roll (or part of a French baguette), which is split lengthways and stuffed with luncheon meats, cheeses, sauces and salads.

Soda: Often refers to a fizzy, sweet, soft-drink

Seltzer: Carbonated, unsweetened water (called 'soda water' in the UK)

Kitty-corner: At a diagonal

Freshman: First year student at high school or university

Sophomore: Second year student in high school or university

Junior: Third year student in high school or university

Senior: Final year student in high school or university

Write an amazing thing you've discovered in here

The NYC Subway system is one of the oldest and largest in the world – with over 400 stations in operation!

The American Museum of Natural History (pg 7) houses a piece of a meteorite that fell in Greenland. Although the bit that is in the museum is only 1/5th of the original, it is so big that it weighs 34 tons and has to be supported by columns driven into the bedrock under the museum!

The tallest building in NYC is the Empire State Building (see pg 19). Each February, there is a race called the Empire State Run-up, where 315 participants run up to the 86th floor observatory — a total of 1,576 heart-pounding steps! The record for the fastest ascent was set way back in 2003, when an Australian guy ran it in 9 minutes and 33 seconds!

There's a statue of a Husky dog called Balto, in Central Park. He's famous because in 1925 he saved many lives by leading a team of sled dogs on a 700 mile journey through a blizzard to deliver some urgently needed medicine to Nome, Alaska.

▲ Write an interesting fact you find in here

MAKE A NOTE

Make a note of your best NYC memories and experiences here!

yum!

COOL

DO A DOODLE

WEIRD & WONDERFUL

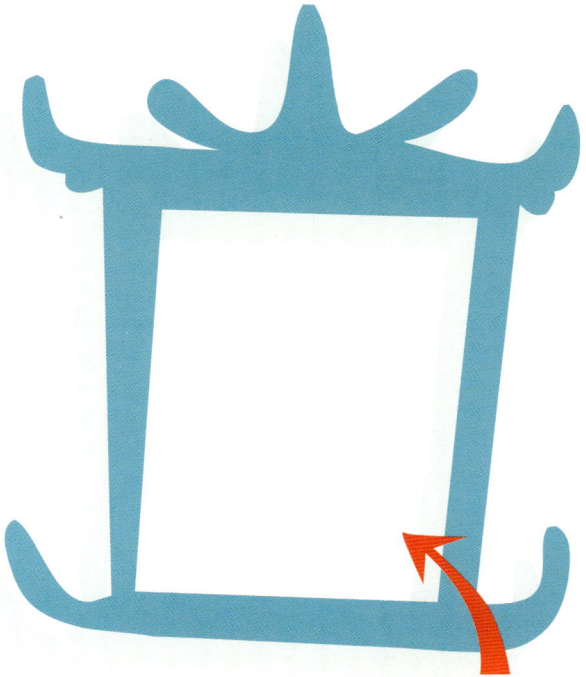

Sketch

KEEPSAKES

Glue your NYC pictures and tickets here!

fun!

WOW

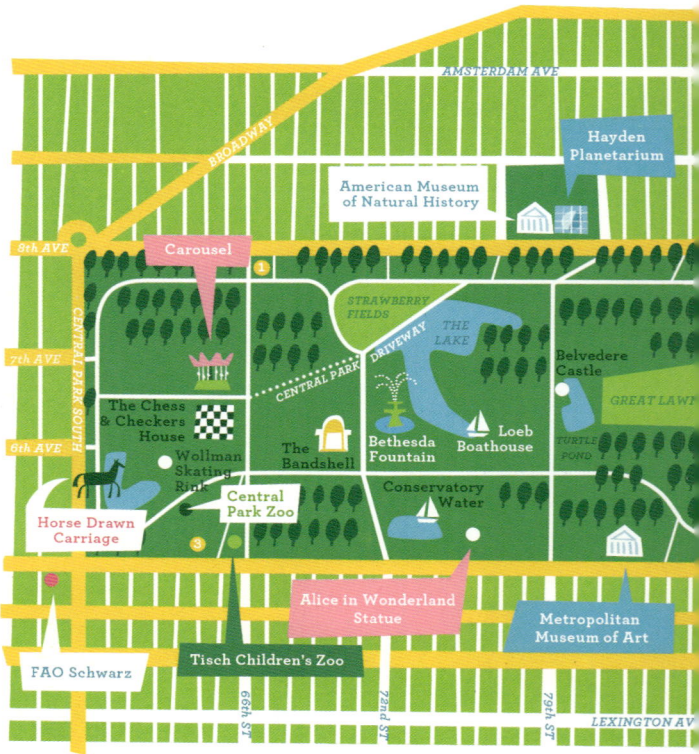

Map labels:
- AMSTERDAM AVE
- Hayden Planetarium
- BROADWAY
- American Museum of Natural History
- 9th AVE
- Carousel
- STRAWBERRY FIELDS
- THE LAKE
- CENTRAL PARK DRIVEWAY
- Belvedere Castle
- 7th AVE
- GREAT LAWN
- CENTRAL PARK SOUTH
- The Chess & Checkers House
- Bethesda Fountain
- Loeb Boathouse
- 6th AVE
- TURTLE POND
- Wollman Skating Rink
- The Bandshell
- Horse Drawn Carriage
- Central Park Zoo
- Conservatory Water
- Alice in Wonderland Statue
- FAO Schwarz
- Tisch Children's Zoo
- Metropolitan Museum of Art
- 66th ST
- 72nd ST
- 79th ST
- LEXINGTON AV

NOT JUST ANY OLD PARK

There are 21 **playgrounds** and more than 20 **sculptures** that you can climb on and explore. Our favorite sculpture is the one of Alice in Wonderland (see map), but a close second is the statue of Balto, the heroic sled-dog (see pg 55). You'll find Balto near the **Tisch Children's Zoo**, at 67th St. During the summer, you can often see concerts and plays around the park, on the **Strawberry Fields**, the **Great Lawn**, in the **Delacorte Theater**, and other places.

VTRAL PARK

86th ST
W. 90th ST
COLUMBUS AVE
110th ST
MANHATTAN AVE
8th AVE
WEST DRIVE
7th AVE
JACQUELINE KENNEDY ONASSIS RESERVOIR
CENTRAL PARK NORTH
LENOX AVE
2
Lasker Rink and Pool
EAST DRIVE
5TH AVE
5th AVE
MADISON AVE
PARK AVE
Solomon R Guggenheim Museum
97th ST

For more information on what's going on, visit an information kiosk or one of the Visitor Centers, such as the **Tavern on the Green Center** 1, the **Chess & Checkers House**, Belvedere Castle or the **Charles A. Dana Discovery Center** 2, where you can also borrow rods and bait to do some fishing in the summer. There are also interesting buildings to investigate – including **Belvedere Castle**, and the **Arsenal** 3.

See other Central Park activity ideas on pg 22.

NEW YORK MAP

Explore & Experience

1. Central Park Zoo p5
2. Roosevelt Island p20
3. Rockefeller Center p4
4. Madame Tussauds & Ripley's Believe It or Not p27
5. New Victory Theater p16
6. Grand Central Terminal p19
7. Madison Square Garden p17
8. Empire State Building p19, 55
9. High Line Park p23
10. Animazing Gallery p28
11. Battery Park p9
12. Staten Island Ferry Pier p6, 8

QUEENS

Citi Field Ball Park
NY Hall of Science
Queens County Farm Museum
Alley Pond Park
Adventure Course Zipline

QUEENSBORO BRIDGE

BRONX
Botanical Gardens
Bronx Zoo
EAST HARLEM

UPPER EAST SIDE

CENTRAL PARK

MORNINGSIDE HEIGHTS

UPPER WEST SIDE

110TH ST.

96TH ST.

59TH ST.

HUDSON RIVER